Stone Town

East Africa,

POCKET TRAVEL GUIDE

2024

© 2024 [Corey M. Webb]

All rights reserved.

No part of this publication may be reproduced, distributed, or transmitted in any form or by any means, including photocopying, recording, or other electronic or mechanical methods, without the prior written permission of the publisher, except in the case of brief quotations embodied in critical reviews and certain other noncommercial uses permitted by copyright law.

Disclaimer:

The information contained in this book is for general information purposes only and is not intended to be a substitute for professional advice. While every effort has been made to ensure the accuracy and completeness of the information contained herein, the author and publisher disclaim any liability for any errors or omissions that may have been made.

Acknowledgments

Webb-Star Guild
"travel the world faster with a pen"

TABLE OF CONTENTS

INTRODUCTION	**6**
Chapter 1: Introduction to Stone Town	**9**
Overview of Stone Town's history and significance	11
Cultural and historical highlights	12
Key landmarks and attractions	13
Chapter 2: Getting to Stone Town: Your Gateway to Zanzibari Magic	**15**
Transportation options:	15
Pro tip: Tips for Smooth Travel to Zanzibar:	17
Visa and entry requirements:	18
How to pack: Travel tips for smooth sailing:	19
Chapter 3: Finding Your Zanzibar Home Away from Home:	**21**
Budget options:	21
Mid-Range Marvels:	23
Luxury Lodgings:	25
Private Island Paradises:	25
Additional Tips:	26
Chapter 4: Unveiling Stone Town's Treasures: Exploring the Sights	**28**
Must-See Masterpieces:	28
More Insider's Off-the-Beaten-Path:	31
Chapter 5: Dining with Delight: Savoring Zanzibar's Flavorful Feast	**34**
Must-Try Classics:	35
Seafood Sensations:	35
Where to Find Your Foodie Bliss:	36

Chapter 6: Island Adventures: Activities and Excursions in Zanzibar   **38**
    Ocean Adventures!   38
    Beyond the Beach Bliss: 40
    Day Trippin' and Excursions Delights: 41
    Cultural Gems and Festivals: 44

Chapter 7:   **46**

Chapter 8: Language and Useful tips   **56**
    Health and Safety Guidance   57
    Emergency Contacts   58
        Medical Emergencies: 59
        Additional Resources: 59
    Local Customs and Etiquette   60
    Common Swahili Phrases for Travelers   61
        Handy Phrases for Various Situations   61

Conclusion   **63**

INTRODUCTION

Welcome to Stone Town, Zanzibar: Where History Meets Turquoise Tides

Jambo! Zama! Hey there! No matter how you say hello, one thing's for sure: Stone Town, Zanzibar is about to weave its magic on you. Buckle up, because this ain't your average travel guide. I'm more like your friendly neighborhood expat, here to share the island's secrets, spiced with a dash of my own adventures.

Think Zanzibar and what pops into your head? Probably palm trees swaying over turquoise waters, right? Spot on! But Stone Town is more than just a beach bum's paradise. It's a labyrinth of narrow alleys, ancient Swahili architecture, and a history richer than the spices that once filled its bustling harbor.

Now, I'm not gonna lie, getting lost in Stone Town's maze-like streets is part of the charm. But let me tell you a quick story. On my first visit, I was map-obsessed, determined to conquer every twist and turn. Big mistake. Ended up spending an hour befriending a local mama who, bless her soul, finally led me back to my hostel, giggling the whole way. Lesson learned: embrace the wanderlust, and you might just stumble upon hidden gems like that hole-in-the-wall serving the best Zanzibari coffee you'll ever sip.

So, what's this little guidebook all about? It's your passport to unlocking the soul of Stone Town. We'll delve into the heart of the Old Town, where crumbling coral houses whisper tales of sultans and explorers. We'll haggle for souvenirs in the bustling markets, where colors explode and aromas dance in the air. We'll savor the freshest seafood at sunset, sand between our toes, and laughter echoing in the balmy Zanzibar breeze.

But this ain't just a sightseeing tour. It's about soaking up the Stone Town vibe. We'll chat with friendly locals, learn a few Swahili phrases (hakuna matata!), and maybe even try our hand at drumming under the starlit sky. Because Stone Town isn't just a place you visit; it's a place you experience.

Chapter 1: Introduction to Stone Town

Stone Town, Zanzibar is a captivating and historic town located on the west coast of Unguja Island, Zanzibar. It is the capital of Zanzibar City and the largest city in Zanzibar. Stone Town is a UNESCO World Heritage Site and is known for its unique architecture, vibrant culture, and rich history. Stone Town's name evolved organically alongside its history and architectural transformation. Here are the key factors that contributed to its moniker:

1. The Dominance of Coral Stone: As mentioned earlier, the widespread use of coral stone became a defining characteristic of the city. Buildings constructed from this readily available and durable material contrasted starkly with the surrounding palm trees and sandy beaches, earning it the nickname "Stone Town" amongst locals and traders.

2. Distinction from Other Zanzibari Settlements: Prior to its widespread stone construction, the area now known as Stone Town was simply referred to as Zanzibar City or Mgongoni (meaning "coconut grove"). As the stone buildings progressively dominated the landscape, it naturally distinguished itself from other settlements on the island, leading to the adoption of "Stone Town" as a unique identifier.

3. Linguistic Fusion: Over time, the Swahili term "Mji Mkongwe" (meaning "Old Town") also emerged to refer to Stone Town, specifically distinguishing it from newer developments in Zanzibar City. However, the moniker "Stone Town" held strong due to its descriptive nature and widespread use by both locals and foreigners.

4. The Power of Simplicity: Unlike "Mji Mkongwe," which required some Swahili knowledge, "Stone Town" was easily understood by traders and travelers from diverse backgrounds. This practical advantage further cemented its usage and spread its fame beyond the island's shores.

Therefore, "Stone Town" emerged as a natural and descriptive name, reflecting the city's distinctive architectural character and evolving identity. It stands as a testament to the enduring legacy of coral stone and the rich cultural tapestry woven into the very fabric of this captivating island paradise.

Overview of Stone Town's history and significance

Stone Town was founded in the 10th century by Arab traders. It quickly became an important center of trade, and by the 19th century, it was one of the most important ports in East Africa. Stone Town was ruled by the Omani Sultanate for over 200 years, and this is reflected in the town's architecture, which is a blend of Arabic, Persian, and Indian influences.

In 1890, Zanzibar became a British protectorate, and Stone Town remained an important port city. However, after independence in 1963, the importance of Stone Town declined. In recent years, Stone Town has undergone a revival, and it is now a popular tourist destination.

Stone Town is a significant place for a number of reasons. It is a UNESCO World Heritage Site, and it is home to a number of important cultural and historical landmarks. Stone Town is also a vibrant and diverse community, and it is a great place to experience the culture of Zanzibar.

Cultural and historical highlights

Stone Town is a fascinating place to explore, and there are many cultural and historical highlights to discover. Some of the most popular attractions include:

- The Old Fort: This 17th-century fort was built by the Omani Sultanate and is now a museum.

- The House of Wonders: This is the largest and most impressive house in Stone Town. It was built in the late 19th century for Sultan Barghash bin Said.
- The Palace Museum: This was the former palace of the Sultans of Zanzibar. It is now a museum that houses a collection of Zanzibar's history and culture.
- The Old Dispensary: This is the oldest building in Stone Town and was originally used as a dispensary for the Omani Sultanate.
- The Anglican Cathedral: This is the oldest church in Stone Town and was built in the 18th century.
- The Forodhani Gardens: These gardens are located on the waterfront and are a popular spot for locals and tourists alike.

Key landmarks and attractions

In addition to the cultural and historical highlights, there are also a number of other key landmarks and attractions in Stone Town. These include:

- The Zanzibar Spice Market: This is a must-visit for any foodie, as it is home to a wide variety of spices, fruits, and vegetables.
- The Zanzibar Stone Town Food Tours: These tours are a great way to sample the local cuisine and learn about the history and culture of Stone Town.
- The Zanzibar Dhow Sailing Tours: These tours are a great way to see Stone Town from a different perspective and to experience the local way of life.
- The Zanzibar Prison: This is a former prison that is now a museum. It is a sobering reminder of Zanzibar's history.
- The Zanzibar Livingstone's House: This is the house where the famous explorer Dr. David Livingstone stayed while he was in Zanzibar. It is now a museum that tells the story of his life and work.

Chapter 2: Getting to Stone Town: Your Gateway to Zanzibari Magic

Mambo jambo! Now that you're hooked on the magic of Stone Town, let's tackle the practicalities of getting there. Buckle up, wanderlust warriors, because we're about to navigate the skies, seas, and maybe even some bumpy roads on our way to paradise.

Transportation options:

Soaring through the skies:

- Zanzibar International Airport (ZNZ): Your most likely landing point, 7km from Stone Town. Plenty of taxis and airport shuttles await, or pre-arrange a transfer for peace of mind.
- Dar es Salaam International Airport (DAR): A larger airport with more flight options, but a 2-hour ferry ride separates you from Stone

Town. Perfect if you fancy a seafaring adventure!

Cruising the azure waves:

- Sea: Ferry your way to Zanzibar! From Dar es Salaam, hop on a passenger ferry or a speedboat for a scenic journey across the turquoise waters. They are generally affordable and scenic, with multiple daily departures. Buckle up for a 2-hour journey, soak in the ocean views, and maybe even spot some playful dolphins.

  Bonus: Enjoy the island's first glimpse as you approach!

- Road: Feeling adventurous? Hire a car from Dar es Salaam and drive across the Nyerere Bridge, a marvel connecting mainland Tanzania to Zanzibar. Remember, left-hand traffic and slower island vibes await!

- Dhows: Traditional wooden sailing vessels offering a romantic, slow-paced journey from nearby islands like Pemba. Perfect for soaking up the sun and Instagram-worthy ocean vistas.

Hitting the road (sometimes):

- Buses from mainland Tanzania: Budget-friendly but can be long and bumpy. Consider overnight options for maximum sleep and minimal road woes.
- Taxis: A convenient but pricier option for short distances. Negotiate fares beforehand and enjoy the ride through charming villages.

Pro tip: Tips for Smooth Travel to Zanzibar:

- Time your arrival: Avoid peak season (July-August) if you prefer quieter streets and lower prices. Shoulder seasons (May-June, September-October) offer pleasant weather and smaller crowds.

- Currency exchange: USD and Euros are widely accepted, but having some Tanzanian Shillings (TSH) is handy for local purchases. ATMs are available in Stone Town.
- Travel insurance: Accidents happen, so consider getting travel insurance for peace of mind.
- Embrace island time: Zanzibar operates on a relaxed schedule. Don't be surprised if things move a bit slower than you're used to. Breathe, unwind, and enjoy island vibes!

Visa and entry requirements:

- Most nationalities require a visa: Apply online or upon arrival. US dollars are preferred for visa fees.
- Valid passport: Make sure it has at least six months of validity remaining.
- Yellow fever vaccination certificate: Mandatory for most travelers.

How to pack: Travel tips for smooth sailing:

- Pack light: Beachwear, comfortable clothes, and a good sunhat are essentials. Leave the bulky winter wardrobe at home!
- Pack for heat: Zanzibar is a tropical paradise, so prepare for sunshine, humidity, and occasional showers.
- Embrace the island pace: Things move a little slower here, so relax, unwind, and savor the laid-back vibes.
- Learn some Swahili: Basic greetings and phrases will go a long way in winning over the friendly locals.
- Bring local currency: While some places accept dollars or euros, Tanzanian shillings are still king. ATMs are readily available in Stone Town.

Remember:

- Double-check visa and entry requirements closer to your travel date, as regulations can change.
- Travel insurance is always a wise investment, especially for unexpected delays or medical emergencies.

Pack your adventurous spirit and infectious curiosity, Stone Town is waiting to charm your socks off!

Chapter 3: Finding Your Zanzibar Home Away from Home:

Where to Stay in Stone Town

Stone Town's charm extends beyond its historic streets and vibrant culture. Finding the perfect place to lay your head after a day of exploration is part of the Zanzibar magic. Whether you're a shoestring backpacker, a luxurious glamper, or a couple seeking a romantic retreat, Stone Town has a little bit of everything. So, grab your imaginary seashells (or earplugs, if you're a light sleeper!), because we're diving into the world of Zanzibari accommodation!

Budget options:

Dhows & Dorms:

Mizingani Seafront Zanzibar: This beachfront hostel boasts a vibrant atmosphere, shared dorms with ocean views, and a rooftop bar for sunset cocktails. Budget-friendly and perfect for social butterflies.

Stone Town Backpackers: Located in the heart of Stone Town, this hostel offers comfortable dorms, a rooftop terrace with city views, and a friendly atmosphere perfect for meeting fellow travelers.

Homestays:

Mama Khadija's Homestay: Experience authentic Zanzibar hospitality at this family-run homestay. Enjoy delicious home-cooked meals, learn Swahili phrases with your hosts, and feel like part of the local community.

Spice House Homestay: Immerse yourself in Zanzibar's spice trade at this unique homestay within a historic spice house. Learn about traditional uses, sleep amidst the fragrant aroma, and enjoy a truly immersive experience.

Budget Boutique Hostels:

The Exchange Zanzibar: This stylish hostel features a mix of dorms and private rooms, a rooftop pool with stunning views, and a trendy bar for social gatherings. Affordable comfort with a modern twist.

Zanzibar Queen Hostel: This vibrant hostel offers themed dorms, a rooftop cinema, and a lively bar scene. Perfect for budget-conscious travelers who want to experience the social side of Zanzibar.

Mid-Range Marvels:

Spice Traders' Retreats:

Emerson Spice Hotel: This restored merchant house features Swahili-style architecture, a courtyard swimming pool, and a rooftop restaurant with panoramic views. Ideal for history buffs who appreciate comfort and style.

The Swahili House: This charming hotel offers intimate rooms with traditional decor, a plunge pool, and a rooftop terrace for relaxing evenings. Perfect for couples seeking a romantic and authentic Zanzibar experience.

Beachside Bungalows:

Sunset Beach Bungalows: Situated right on Kendwa Beach, these bungalows offer private balconies with ocean views, a beachfront restaurant, and a relaxed atmosphere. Perfect for those who crave sun, sand, and barefoot luxury.

Matemwe Beach Bungalows: Nestled on Matemwe Beach, these bungalows offer spacious rooms with ocean views, a swimming pool, and a spa. Ideal for families or groups seeking a peaceful beach escape.

Charming Boutique Hotels:

Zanzi House: This intimate hotel features stylish rooms with balconies, a rooftop pool with city views, and a rooftop restaurant serving delicious local cuisine. Perfect for those seeking a personalized and stylish stay in Stone Town.

The Manor House: This historic mansion offers elegant rooms with antique furniture, a charming courtyard with a plunge pool, and a rooftop terrace for sunset drinks. Ideal for travelers who appreciate old-world charm and a touch of luxury.

Luxury Lodgings:

The Zanzibar Palace Hotel: This restored palace offers opulent suites with ocean views, a private infinity pool, and personalized butler service. Live like royalty and experience the ultimate Zanzibar indulgence.

Mtoni Marine Hotel: This beachfront resort boasts luxurious villas with private pools, a spa, and gourmet dining. Perfect for honeymooners or those seeking an unforgettable retreat.

Private Island Paradises:

Chumbe Island Coral Lodge: This eco-friendly resort on a private island offers luxurious bungalows with ocean views, snorkeling and diving excursions, and a commitment to sustainable tourism. Ideal for nature lovers and those seeking a truly unique experience.

Mnemba Island Lodge: This exclusive resort on a tiny island offers private beachfront villas with infinity pools, gourmet dining, and personalized service. The ultimate private island escape for discerning travelers.

Remember: These are just a few examples, and Stone Town offers a vast array of accommodation options to suit every budget and style. Don't hesitate to explore further and find a place that truly speaks to your Zanzibar dream!

Additional Tips:

- Consider using online booking platforms like Booking.com or Airbnb to compare prices and read guest reviews.
- Think about your location preferences. Do you want to be in the heart of Stone Town, close to the action, or on a quiet beach?
- Don't hesitate to ask locals for recommendations. They often have hidden gems up their sleeves!

Chapter 4: Unveiling Stone Town's Treasures: Exploring the Sights

Habari gani, explorers! Zanzibar's magic isn't just about sun-kissed beaches and turquoise waters. Stone Town, its heart and soul, pulsates with history, culture, and hidden gems waiting to be unearthed. So, dust off your curiosity, grab your trusty map (or embrace the thrill of getting lost!), and let's dive into the labyrinthine streets of Stone Town, unearthing its captivating sights:

Must-See Masterpieces:

The House of Wonders: This architectural marvel, once the Sultan's palace, now houses the National Museum of Zanzibar. Explore the opulent halls, marvel at intricate carvings, and delve into the island's rich history.

Stone Town Old Dispensary: This quirky building, with its vibrant facade and Zanzibar's first pharmacy, is a photographer's dream. Peek inside, catch the light filtering through stained glass windows, and capture a piece of Stone Town's charm.

Forodhani Gardens: As the sun dips below the horizon, this waterfront park comes alive with vibrant energy. Savor fresh seafood at bustling food stalls, mingle with locals, and witness the mesmerizing sunset paint the sky in fiery hues.

Anglican Cathedral: This imposing cathedral, built on the site of a former slave market, stands as a poignant symbol of Zanzibar's past. Explore its Gothic architecture, learn about its history, and pay resCultural & Heritage Delights:

Stone Town Historical Tours: Join a guided walk through Stone Town's labyrinthine streets and discover hidden alleys, ancient doorways, and fascinating stories of sultans, explorers, and everyday life.

Dhow Building Yard: Witness the craftsmanship behind Zanzibar's traditional dhows at this historic boatyard. Learn about the construction process, admire the intricate carvings, and feel the pulse of the island's maritime heritage.

Old Slave Market: Witness a poignant piece of Zanzibar's history at the Old Slave Market. Learn about the island's role in the slave trade, pay tribute to those who suffered, and reflect on the importance of freedom and unity.

Sultan's Palace: Step into the grand palace of Zanzibar's sultans, now a fascinating museum. Explore intricately carved doors, admire priceless artifacts, and imagine the opulent lives of those who once ruled the island.

Livingstone's House: Visit the former home of the famous explorer Dr. David Livingstone, where he prepared for his expeditions into Africa. Learn about his adventures and the impact he had on Zanzibar.

Changuu Island, where a former prison now shelters giant tortoises. Explore the ruins, peek into the prison cells, and learn about the island's fascinating history. Don't forget to snap a selfie with the resident giants – they're quite camera-friendly!

More Insider's Off-the-Beaten-Path:

Emerson Spice House: Immerse yourself in Zanzibar's aromatic heritage at this hidden gem. Learn about traditional spice uses, grind your own blends, and fill your suitcase with fragrant souvenirs.

Memories of Zanzibar: Step into a world of Zanzibar's vibrant art scene at this tucked-away gallery. Discover local artists, admire stunning paintings and sculptures, and maybe even find a unique piece to take home.

Bibi Beach: avoid the tourist crowds and find your own slice of paradise at this secluded beach. Soak up the sun, snorkel in coral reefs, and enjoy the laid-back atmosphere.

Darajani Market: get into the heart of Stone Town's bustling life at this vibrant market. Haggle for souvenirs, sample exotic fruits, and get a glimpse into the daily routines of locals.

Jozani Chwaka Bay National Park: Step into a lush green wonderland, home to playful red colobus monkeys and elusive blue monkeys. Hike through mangroves, kayak through the forest, and marvel at the unique biodiversity of this protected gem.

The Rock Restaurant: Perched on a rocky outcrop, this iconic restaurant offers a culinary and visual feast. Watch the tide rise and fall around your table, savor gourmet seafood as the sun dips below the horizon, and create memories that will last a lifetime.

Nungwi Beach Bliss: Escape the bustle of Stone Town and trade cobbled streets for pristine sands. Nungwi Beach beckons with turquoise waters, swaying palm trees, and a laid-back vibe. Soak up the sun, try your hand at watersports, or simply unwind with a good book and the soothing rhythm of the waves.

Remember, dear traveler:

Respect Local Customs: Zanzibar is a Muslim island. Dress modestly, especially when visiting religious sites.

Support Local Businesses: Opt for locally-owned restaurants, homestays, and tours. Your choice can make a real difference in the lives of Zanzibar's people.

With this guide in hand and a heart full of wonder, you're ready to embark on an unforgettable exploration of Zanzibar's sights. Go forth, discover hidden alleyways, savor cultural treasures, and create memories that will forever shimmer under the Zanzibari sun!

Next stop: Chapter 5: Spice Up Your Zanzibar Adventure! Get ready to delve into the aromatic world of Zanzibari cuisine, cooking classes, and spice markets. Stay tuned!

Chapter 5: Dining with Delight: Savoring Zanzibar's Flavorful Feast

Habari gani, foodies and flavor chasers! Zanzibar's not just an island paradise, it's a culinary wonder! From fragrant spices that whisper ancient secrets to fresh seafood dancing on the grill, get ready to tantalize your taste buds with dishes that burst with sunshine and soul. So, loosen your belts, grab your napkins, and let's dive into the heart of Zanzibar's food scene!

Zanzibar's Flavorful Fusion:

Imagine a symphony of aromas – the heady warmth of cloves, the citrusy zing of coriander, the sweet earthiness of coconut. Zanzibar's cuisine is a unique blend of Arab, Indian, African, and Portuguese influences, each playing a delicious note in the island's culinary orchestra.

Must-Try Classics:

Zanzibar's soul is woven with spices. Dig into a fiery **Pili Pili Chicken**, where chili peppers tango with ginger and coconut milk. Or savor a fragrant **Biryani, rice** layered with spices, meat, and vegetables, a dish fit for sultans!

Seafood Sensations:

Fresh from the turquoise waters, Zanzibar's seafood is a must-try. Dive into a plate of *strong***Octopus Curry**, tender tentacles simmered in a rich coconut sauce. Or indulge in a platter of Zanzibar **Grilled Lobster**, its sweet flesh kissed by flames and basted with garlic butter.

Island Treasures: Don't miss *strong***Mishkakist**, skewers of marinated meat grilled to juicy perfection. And be sure to try **Mandizi**, fluffy fried doughnuts dusted with sugar, the perfect sweet treat for afternoon adventures.

Where to Find Your Foodie Bliss:

Forodhani Gardens: As the sun dips below the horizon, Stone Town's Forodhani Gardens ignite with life and sizzling aromas. Here, friendly vendors tempt your palate with grilled seafood, spiced skewers, and Zanzibar's iconic street food. Grab a stool, mingle with the locals, and let the vibrant energy wash over you.

Mama's Home Cooking: Experience the warmth of Zanzibari hospitality at a local homestay. Mama will whip up a feast of fresh fish, coconut curries, and fragrant rice, all served with a smile and a side of island stories.

The Rock Restaurant: Perched on a rocky outcrop, this iconic restaurant offers a culinary and visual feast. Watch the tide rise and fall around your table as you savor gourmet seafood and sip cocktails under the starlit sky. It's an experience for the senses, and your Instagram followers will thank you!

Embrace the Spice: Don't be afraid to explore the spice stalls in Stone Town Markets. Ask questions, sample exotic powders, and create your own spice blend to take home – a fragrant souvenir of your Zanzibari adventure.

Remember, food is more than just fuel. It's a window into a culture, a way to connect with locals, and a memory that lingers long after your tan fades. So, open your heart, open your senses, and let Zanzibar's cuisine paint your taste buds with sunshine and spice!

Chapter 6: Island Adventures: Activities and Excursions in Zanzibar

Thrill seekers and island hoppers! Zanzibar's calling, and it's got more in store than just sunburnt noses and sandy toes (though those are pretty darn tempting too!). This spice-infused paradise is a playground for the adventurous soul, bursting with opportunities to get your heart pounding, your adrenaline pumping, and your wanderlust meter maxed out. So, grab your snorkel mask, your hiking boots, and that insatiable sense of discovery, because we're about to unleash your inner explorer in Zanzibar!

Ocean Adventures!

Dive into Turquoise Paradise: The coral reefs around Zanzibar are a kaleidoscope of life, teeming with neon fish, swaying anemones, and maybe even a majestic sea turtle cruising by. Whether you're a seasoned aqua-naut or a curious first-timer, there's an underwater adventure waiting to blow your fins off.

Catch a Wave: Feeling the salty spray on your face as you conquer a turquoise wave is a Zanzibar must-do. From gentle beginner lessons to gnarly advanced swells, there's a surfing experience for every level. So grab your board, paddle out, and hang ten like a champ!

Windsurf fun: Harness the island's trade winds and let your sail take flight. Zanzibar's beaches offer epic windsurfing conditions, perfect for carving across the water like a boss and feeling the wind whip through your hair. Trust me, the sunset views from your board are worth every wipeout.

Dolphin Dance: Set sail on a dhow cruise and witness the playful dance of dolphins in their natural habitat. Watch them leap and spin in the sunlight, breathe in the salty air, and let the magic of the Indian Ocean wash over you.

Beyond the Beach Bliss:

Bring your Hike boots!: Lace up your boots and trek through Jozani Chwaka Bay National Park, a lush green haven for playful red colobus monkeys, exotic birdsong, and ancient mangrove forests. Breathe in the fresh air, listen to the symphony of the wild, and witness the island's vibrant ecosystem come alive.

Go Spelunking in Nungwi: Dare to venture into the darkness of Kuza Cave, a natural wonder sculpted by the waves. Explore its hidden chambers, be dazzled by sparkling stalactites, and feel the thrill of discovering this magical underworld. Just remember, bring a headlamp and a healthy dose of adventure!

Biking sure your way to move: Ditch the taxis and hop on a bicycle. Wind through charming villages, explore back roads fringed with palm trees, and stumble upon hidden gems far from the tourist crowds. It's a fantastic way to connect with the island's rhythm and soak in the local beauty at your own pace.

Day Trippin' and Excursions Delights:

Chumbe Island:
You would definitely love to go on a day trip to Chumbe Island Coral Park, a protected marine area

offering exceptional snorkeling opportunities and a chance to explore the island's nature trails.

**Prison Island*:*
Visit the historical Prison Island, home to giant tortoises, and learn about its intriguing past while enjoying the island's natural beauty.

Kizimkazi Cultural and Historical Sites:
Explore the historical ruins and cultural landmarks in Kizimkazi, including the Dimbani Mosque and other points of interest.

Local Markets and Craft Fairs:
Explore the bustling markets of Stone Town, where you can witness traditional crafts, artwork, and local products, providing an authentic cultural experience.

Swahili Cooking Classes and Cultural Workshops:
Participate in Swahili Cooking Classes to learn about local cuisine or engage in cultural workshops that offer insights into traditional music, dance, and art.

Prison Island Escape: Take a boat trip to Changuu Island, where a former prison now shelters giant tortoises with personalities as big as their shells. Explore the ruins, peek into the cells, and learn about the island's fascinating history. Don't forget to snap a selfie with the resident giants – they're quite the camera hogs!

Spice Island Secrets: feel yourself in the heart and soul of Zanzibar at a spice farm. Learn how nutmeg bursts from the trees, how cinnamon curls like fragrant scrolls, and about the ancient uses of these exotic treasures. Grind your own blends, fill your suitcase with aromatic souvenirs, and let the island's spicy secrets leave a lasting impression.

Stone Town Sunset Cruise: As the sun dips below the horizon, paint the sky with fiery hues aboard a traditional dhow. Sail past ancient palaces, watch fishermen cast their nets, and share stories with fellow travelers under the starlit sky. It's an experience that will stay with you long after the last rays of sunlight fade.

Cultural Gems and Festivals:

Rhythms of Mbende: Witness the vibrant Mbende music and dance tradition. Sway to the energetic drumming, clap to the infectious rhythms, and be awestruck by the colorful costumes and mesmerizing movements. Let the music move you and feel the spirit of Zanzibar come alive.

Zanzibar International Film Festival: watch acclaimed documentaries, independent features, and world cinema under the Zanzibari sun. This annual event is a celebration of diverse voices and stories, offering a unique window into global cultures. So grab some popcorn and settle in for a cinematic adventure.

Sauti za Busara Music Festival:

If your visit aligns with the annual Sauti za Busara Music Festival, which takes place over three days in February, and features a variety of musical genres, including Taarab, Afrobeat, hip hop, reggae, and more. In addition to live music, the festival also offers a variety of cultural events, such as dance performances, traditional drumming workshops, and art exhibitions. immerse yourself in a vibrant celebration of African music and cultural performances.

Zanzibar doesn't shy away from a good party! From the vibrant **Eid al-Fitr celebrations** to the joyous harvest festivals, there's always a chance to experience the island's rich cultural tapestry. Immerse yourself in the music, dance, and delicious food, and let the Zanzibari spirit sweep you away. adventure isn't just about ticking off a list.

Chapter 7:

Lets craft your 7-10 days travel itinerary !

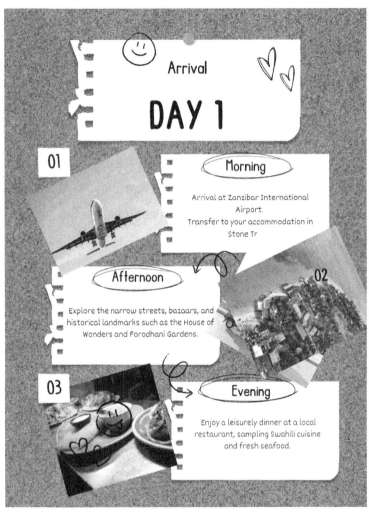

DAY 2

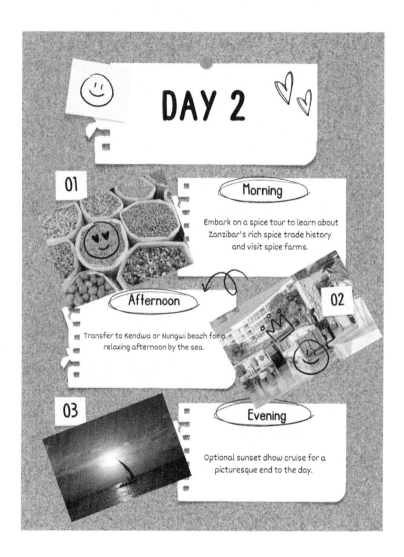

01 Morning
Embark on a spice tour to learn about Zanzibar's rich spice trade history and visit spice farms.

02 Afternoon
Transfer to Kendwa or Nungwi beach for a relaxing afternoon by the sea.

03 Evening
Optional sunset dhow cruise for a picturesque end to the day.

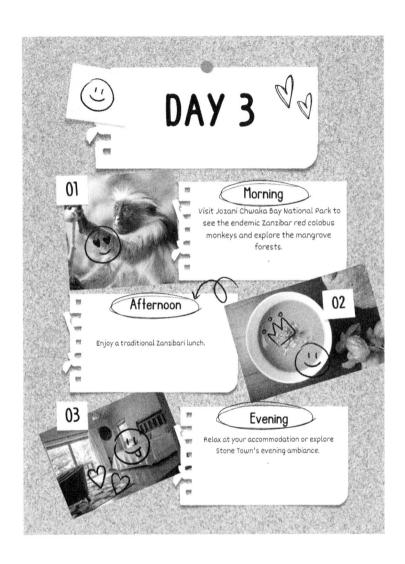

DAY 4

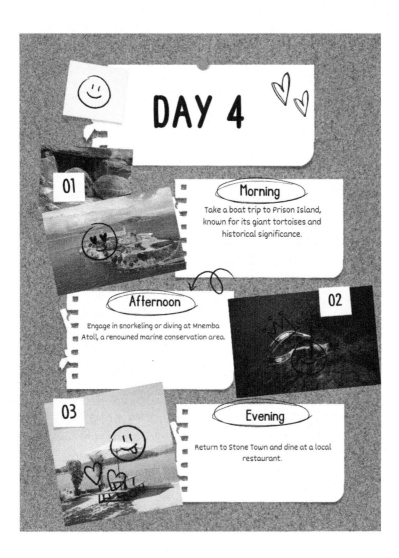

01 Morning
Take a boat trip to Prison Island, known for its giant tortoises and historical significance.

Afternoon 02
Engage in snorkeling or diving at Mnemba Atoll, a renowned marine conservation area.

03 Evening
Return to Stone Town and dine at a local restaurant.

DAY 5

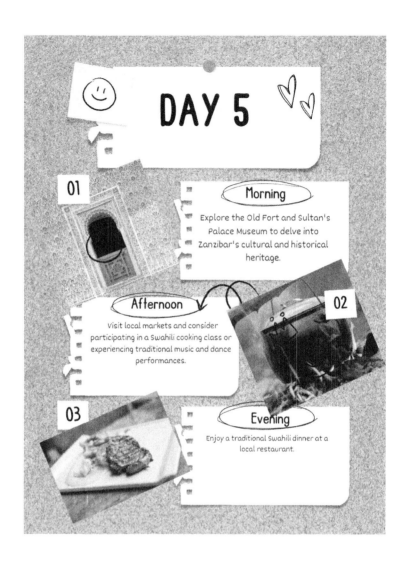

01

Morning

Explore the Old Fort and Sultan's Palace Museum to delve into Zanzibar's cultural and historical heritage.

Afternoon

Visit local markets and consider participating in a Swahili cooking class or experiencing traditional music and dance performances.

02

03

Evening

Enjoy a traditional Swahili dinner at a local restaurant.

DAY 6

01

Morning
Take a day trip to Paje and Jambiani for activities such as kite surfing, beach horseback riding, and exploring the vibrant coastal communities.

Afternoon
Enjoy a beachside lunch.

02

03

Evening
Return to Stone Town and relax at your accommodation.

51

DAY 7

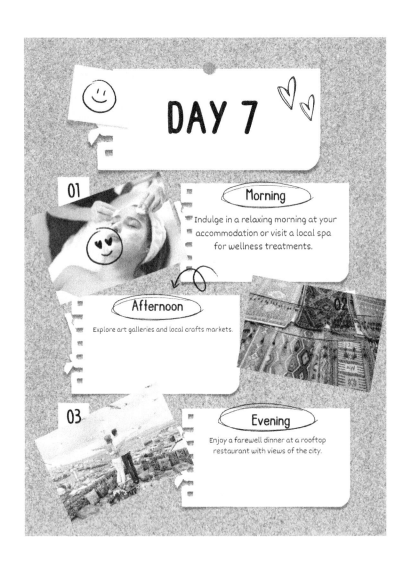

01 Morning
Indulge in a relaxing morning at your accommodation or visit a local spa for wellness treatments.

Afternoon
Explore art galleries and local crafts markets.

03 Evening
Enjoy a farewell dinner at a rooftop restaurant with views of the city.

DAY 8

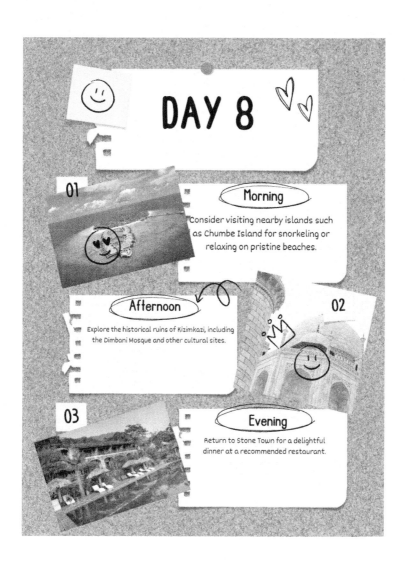

01 Morning
Consider visiting nearby islands such as Chumbe Island for snorkeling or relaxing on pristine beaches.

Afternoon
Explore the historical ruins of Kizimkazi, including the Dimbani Mosque and other cultural sites.

02

03 Evening
Return to Stone Town for a delightful dinner at a recommended restaurant.

DAY 9-10

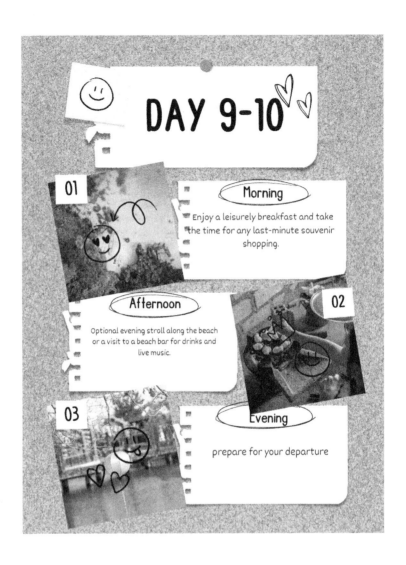

01

Morning
Enjoy a leisurely breakfast and take the time for any last-minute souvenir shopping.

Afternoon
Optional evening stroll along the beach or a visit to a beach bar for drinks and live music.

02

03

Evening
prepare for your departure

54

farewell

have your farewell zanzibari breakfast, watching the city come alive one last time. choosing the right things to remind you of your experience.

Transfer to Zanzibar International Airport for departure.

Chapter 8: Language and Useful tips

When visiting Zanzibar, embracing the local language and customs enhances the overall travel experience, fostering meaningful connections with the community. Here's a comprehensive guide encompassing practical information, travel tips, language essentials, and cultural etiquette.

Practical Information

Currency and Payments**: The official currency in Zanzibar is the Tanzanian shilling. Although most big places happily accept credit cards, it's always a good idea to have some cash on hand for those smaller local sellers and delightful markets.

Transportation**: Utilize reputable taxi services or arrange transportation through trusted providers. Negotiate fares in advance when using local taxis or dala-dalas (minibus taxis).

Weather and Attire**: Zanzibar experiences a tropical climate, so lightweight, breathable clothing is recommended. Respect local customs by dressing modestly when visiting religious sites and rural areas.

Health and Safety Guidance

Medical Facilities**: Familiarize yourself with the locations of medical facilities and pharmacies in your area of stay, and consider obtaining travel insurance for peace of mind.

Water and Food Safety**: Opt for bottled water and ensure that seafood and other perishables are prepared and served at reputable establishments to avoid food-borne illnesses.

Health Precautions**: Stay hydrated and protect against mosquito bites by using repellent and wearing long sleeves during dusk and dawn, when mosquitoes are most active.

Responsible Tourism**: Support sustainable practices by minimizing plastic usage, respecting natural habitats, and engaging in eco-friendly activities such as reef-safe snorkeling.

Respecting Local Customs**: Embrace cultural sensitivity by seeking permission before taking photos of individuals, especially in rural and village settings.

Emergency Contacts

- Emergency Number: 112 (similar to 911)
- Police: 118 or 24 223 0772 (Main Station, Stone Town)
- Fire Department: 111
- Ambulance: 114

- Tanzania Tourist Police: +255 24 223 5669

Medical Emergencies:

- Zanzibar Medical and Diagnostic Centre: 24 223 1071 (24-hour emergency line)
- Mnazi Mmoja Hospital: 24 223 6101
- Bethsaida Government Hospital: 24 223 0266
- House Call Doctors (Private Service): 255 629 227 983

Additional Resources:

- Tanzania Tourist Board: +255 22 211 7233
- US Embassy in Dar es Salaam: +255 22 266 9500
- UK High Commission in Dar es Salaam: +255 22 216 6000

Tips:

- Save these numbers in your phone's contacts for easy access.

- Consider purchasing a local SIM card to ensure reliable phone connectivity.
- Learn basic Swahili phrases like "Msaada!" (Help!) or "Nina dharura!" (I have an emergency!).
- Carry travel insurance and familiarize yourself with its coverage before your trip.
- Stay informed about local conditions and potential safety risks by checking travel advisories and news updates.

Local Customs and Etiquette

Greetings and Courtesies**: Embrace the local custom of greeting with "Jambo" (Hello) and "Asante" (Thank you). Modest behavior and respectful interactions are highly valued in Zanzibari culture.

Respecting Religious Practices**: When visiting mosques and other religious sites, dress modestly, and adhere to guidelines for visitors, such as removing shoes and covering the head for women.

Common Swahili Phrases for Travelers

Greetings
  Jambo - Hello
  Habari - How are you?
  Nzuri - Fine

Basic Phrases
  Asante - Thank you
  Samahani - Excuse me
  Tafadhali - Please

Numbers
  Moja - One
  Mbili - Two
  Tatu - Three

Handy Phrases for Various Situations

At the Market

Nipe bei nzuri - Give me a good price
Ninafanya ununuzi - I am shopping

Asking for Directions
Naweza pata wapi...? - Where can I find...?
Jinsi ya kwenda...? - How do I get to...?

Zanzibar is a place to embrace the warmth and hospitality of its people. A little cultural understanding and a sprinkle of Swahili go a long way in unlocking the island's true magic. So, put your language skills to the test, smile often, and let Zanzibar's vibrant rhythm guide your every step.With this knowledge in your backpack and a heart full of wanderlust, you're ready to truly embrace the spirit of Zanzibar. Moreso, this is just the beginning of your island adventure. Explore, discover, and savor every moment, for Zanzibar's magic is a gift that keeps on giving, long after you leave its shores.

Now, go forth, explore, and let your Zanzibar story unfold!

Conclusion

And so, dear adventurer, your Stone Town adventure awaits! This pocket guide is your Zanzibar whisperer, your map to hidden gems, your sprinkle of Swahili magic to light your way. Lose yourself in labyrinthine streets, haggle with a smile in bustling markets, and let the island's rhythm pulse through your veins. Remember, the most enchanting treasures are often tucked away, so wander with open eyes, embrace the unexpected, and create memories that will shimmer long after you leave.

Share your Zanzibar magic with the world! Drop a review on this guide, become a compass for others, and paint the world with your unique island stories. Habari gani, and may your Stone Town journey be filled with wonder, spice, and sunshine!

Printed in Great Britain
by Amazon